Student Affairs Administrators
in Higher Education

STUDENT WORKBOOK

CERTIFIED PEER EDUCATOR

Version 4.1

Healthy, Safety, and Well-Being Initiatives of NASPA

Published by

NASPA–Student Affairs Administrators in Higher Education
111 K Street, NE
10th Floor
Washington, DC 20002
www.naspa.org

Additional copies may be purchased by contacting the NASPA publications department at 202-265-7500 or visiting http://bookstore.naspa.org.

NASPA does not discriminate on the basis of race, color, national origin, religion, sex, age, gender identity, gender expression, affectional or sexual orientation, or disability in any of its policies, programs, and services.

ISBN 978-1-948213-11-0

Printed and bound in the United States of America

Version 4.1

CONTENTS

STUDENT WORKBOOK

WELCOME FROM NASPA

Dear Peer Educator:

We are excited that you have chosen to embark on a journey to become a Certified Peer Educator (CPE) through the CPE Training Program! You are taking a great step to learn and improve your skills to become an effective friend, educator, activist, role model, and team member.

This training is designed to enhance the skills you need to be effective. We hope that you will actively participate in this course through the vast array of activities we have provided in this workbook. Make sure to ask questions, challenge ideas, and share your thoughts.

This student workbook is yours to keep. It is by no means comprehensive—rather, it is a resource that you can use both during and after the training. It includes worksheets for you to use during this training course as well as sample worksheets in the appendices section for you to use in the future.

At the conclusion of the training, you will complete the CPE Certification Test. After successfully completing the test, you will receive your certification materials and join more than 300,000 of your peers who have been certified through the CPE Program since its launch in 1994.

Thank you again for your commitment, and we look forward to certifying you! The students, environments, and quality of life on our campuses and in our communities will be enhanced because of you!

Sincerely,

Jason Davis
Assistant Director of Peer Education Initiatives and Training Programs
NASPA–Student Affairs Administrators in Higher Education

ACKNOWLEDGMENTS

This edition of the NASPA CPE Training Program was developed from a wonderful foundation laid by long-time volunteers as well as input from NASPA staff and volunteers. We would like to thank those individuals for their time, expertise, and dedication to making this project a success.

HEALTH, SAFETY, AND WELL-BEING INITIATIVES OF NASPA STAFF

David Arnold
Jason Davis
Maureen Dechico
Sarice Greenstein
Laurie Jevons

Mallory Jordan
Allison Tombros Korman
Rachael Novick
Emma Spalding

ADDITIONAL NASPA STAFF

Melissa Dahne
Jill Dunlap
Stephanie Gordon
Jace Kirschner

Kevin Kruger
Amelia Parnell
Jasmine Scott
Amy Shopkorn

STUDENT WORKBOOK

VOLUNTEER CONTRIBUTORS

Kristelle Aisaka
Olga Antonio
Jay Cutspec
Eric Garrison
Nicole Giglia
Slade Gormus
Lauren Kaplan

Whitney O'Regan
Michelle Sloan
Grace Turner
Brian Vanderheyden
Brittney Vigna
Alex Washburn

ADDITIONAL ACKNOWLEDGMENTS

We would like to thank Shawn Hann and the Denver School for the Arts for collaborating with us on video production. In addition, we appreciate the actors and members of the Fireside Production team who were integral to the process.

Sofie Berg
Naomi Binkley
Victor Castroverde
Hattie Hodes
Yasmine Hunter
Miranda Martinez

Kristin Massoletti
Thomas McDonald
Kala Montoya
TJ Morgan
SaDaiveon Newell
Abby Stuckrath

Finally, we recognize that the CPE Training Program has a long legacy and has existed in many iterations. We would like to thank those individuals who have dedicated their time and expertise to work on past editions of the CPE curriculum.

JM Alatis
Janet Cox
Lisa Currie
Eric Davidson
Ann Doyle
Jan Gascoigne
Marc Goldfarb
David Hellstrom
Drew Hunter
Kari Kuka

Amy Lukowski
Michael McNeill
Amy Melichar
Miriam Nicklaus
Laurel Okasaki-Cardos
Ann Quinn-Zobeck
Nikki Smith
Tony Thomson
Andrea Zelinko

PEER EDUCATOR CODE OF ETHICS

I value and know my role as a peer educator.
In order to best fulfill that role, I will:
Grant individuals respect and dignity;
Honor and strive to understand diversity in all its forms;
Recognize that, through patience and understanding, every person is constantly growing and learning.

I value and know my role as a friend.
In order to best fulfill that role, I will:
Offer opportunities for people to explore their thoughts and feelings;
Offer myself as a link between students and the professional services on campus or in the community;
Not manipulate any situation or another person's vulnerability for my own benefit;
Maintain confidentiality, except when, to my best judgment, the person is in physical or mental danger that could result in self-harm or harm to others, has a problem beyond my ability to assist, or discloses information that I must report according to law or campus policy.

I value and know my role as an educator.
In order to best fulfill that role, I will:
Learn as much as possible about the issues that affect my peers;
Offer only information that I am qualified to offer and with the greatest accuracy possible;
Accept feedback and support from my advisor, supervisor, or other professional staff.

I value and know my role as an activist.
In order to best fulfill that role, I will:
Refuse to be a passive bystander;
Confront unhealthy attitudes and behaviors;
Work to change the campus and community environment to promote healthy choices.

cpe
Certified Peer Educator

I value and know my role as a role model.
In order to best fulfill that role, I will:
Make decisions in my own life that are positive and healthy;
Challenge myself to continue my own physical, mental, and emotional growth;
Accept guidance and feedback from others who care about me.

I value and know my role as a team member.
In order to best fulfill that role, I will:
Accept supervision and support from my advisor;
Commit to actively participating in the peer education group;
Support and encourage my fellow peer educators.

I value and know my role as an individual.
In order to best fulfill this role, I will:
Understand my primary responsibility is to myself;
Not allow my peer education duties to interfere with my own goals and aspirations;
Not allow my role as a peer educator to put my emotional, mental, or physical well-being at risk.

CPE COURSE LEARNING OUTCOMES

MODULE 1

- Students will define the five roles of an individual peer educator.
- Students will recognize common traps that peer educators may fall into.
- Students will learn the Peer Educator Code of Ethics.
- Students will define healthy and balanced living as a learner and peer educator.
- Students will identify healthy strategies for self-care.
- Students will define both eustress and distress.

MODULE 2

- Students will be able to describe ways to create change in various environments using the social ecological model.
- Students will be able to apply each of the five stages of the Transtheoretical Model.
- Students will discuss the Diffusion of Innovations Model and its application to their role as peer educators.

MODULE 3

- Students will be able to identify characteristics of a good listener.
- Students will be able to identify barriers to good listening.
- Students will apply techniques of listening effectively and encouraging individuals to share.
- Students will reflect on their nonverbal communication.
- Students will practice their own listening skills.

MODULE 4

- Students will reflect on the distinction between confidentiality and privacy.
- Students will develop skills to help their peers establish a plan of action when they are in distress.

- Students will determine when referrals are needed when dealing with a peer in distress.
- Students will increase their knowledge of professional, campus, and community resources available to those affected by crisis.

MODULE 5

- Students will be able to define active and passive bystanders.
- Students will be able to describe factors of ambivalence related to bystander intervention.
- Students will reflect on personal barriers that could cause them to be a passive bystander.

MODULE 6

- Students will identify the difference between personal and social identities.
- Students will gain a basic understanding of privileged and historically disenfranchised identities.

MODULE 7

- Students will practice program planning.
- Students will write learning outcomes and objectives.
- Students will examine different methods of presentation planning through the four cornerstones and three parts of successful presentations.
- Students will reflect on different evaluation strategies for program planning and presentations.

MODULE 8

- Students will be able to identify the components of the basic cycle of group formation and development.
- Students will understand the role of their advisor/supervisor to achieve the team's goals.
- Students will understand ways to appreciate and recognize achievements of both the group and individual members.
- Students will develop or reexamine their group's mission and vision.
- Students will discuss habits of highly effective peer education groups.

CPE PRETEST

You are encouraged to begin the course by completing the CPE Pretest online. If you choose to not log in to the NASPA Online Learning Community to establish your account prior to beginning the training, please answer the following CPE Pretest questions.

These questions are not graded and will have no bearing on your ability to complete the course. You will be asked to transpose these questions to the online certification website prior to completing the CPE Program.

QUESTION 1

Rate your level of knowledge about the following:

Acting with ethics and integrity

Answer (select one):

☐ No knowledge

☐ Little knowledge

☑ Adequate knowledge

☐ Extraordinary knowledge

QUESTION 2

Rate your level of knowledge about the following:

The roles peer educators play on campus

Answer (select one):

- ☐ No knowledge
- ☑ Little knowledge
- ☐ Adequate knowledge
- ☐ Extraordinary knowledge

QUESTION 3

Rate your level of knowledge about the following:

Strategies for facilitating behavior change

Answer (select one):

- ☐ No knowledge
- ☐ Little knowledge
- ☑ Adequate knowledge
- ☐ Extraordinary knowledge

QUESTION 4

Rate your level of knowledge about the following:

The process through which change happens on a community level

Answer (select one):

- ☐ No knowledge
- ☑ Little knowledge
- ☐ Adequate knowledge
- ☐ Extraordinary knowledge

QUESTION 5

Rate your level of knowledge about the following:

Techniques for active listening

Answer (select one):

- ☐ No knowledge
- ☐ Little knowledge
- ☑ Adequate knowledge
- ☐ Extraordinary knowledge

QUESTION 6

Rate your level of knowledge about the following:

Barriers to active listening

Answer (select one):

- ☐ No knowledge
- ☐ Little knowledge
- ☑ Adequate knowledge
- ☐ Extraordinary knowledge

QUESTION 7

Rate your level of knowledge about the following:

Ways to encourage individuals to share when speaking to them

Answer (select one):

- ☐ No knowledge
- ☐ Little knowledge
- ☑ Adequate knowledge
- ☐ Extraordinary knowledge

QUESTION 8

Rate your level of knowledge about the following:

Campus resources and how to refer students

Answer (select one):

- ☐ No knowledge
- ☐ Little knowledge
- ☐ Adequate knowledge
- ☑ Extraordinary knowledge

QUESTION 9

Rate your level of knowledge about the following:

Creating a plan of action to help a student deal with a **distressing situation**

Answer (select one):

- ☐ No knowledge
- ☐ Little knowledge
- ☐ Adequate knowledge
- ☑ Extraordinary knowledge

QUESTION 10

Rate your level of knowledge about the following:

How to intervene safely and effectively as a bystander

Answer (select one):

- ☐ No knowledge
- ☐ Little knowledge
- ☑ Adequate knowledge
- ☐ Extraordinary knowledge

QUESTION 11

Rate your level of knowledge about the following:

Your own social identities

Answer (select one):

- ☐ No knowledge
- ☑ Little knowledge
- ☐ Adequate knowledge
- ☐ Extraordinary knowledge

QUESTION 12

Rate your level of knowledge about the following:

The ways in which social identities might affect your work as a peer educator

Answer (select one):

- ☐ No knowledge
- ☑ Little knowledge
- ☐ Adequate knowledge
- ☐ Extraordinary knowledge

QUESTION 13

Rate your level of knowledge about the following:

Steps needed to plan a successful program

Answer (select one):

- ☐ No knowledge
- ☑ Little knowledge
- ☐ Adequate knowledge
- ☐ Extraordinary knowledge

cpe
Certified Peer Educator

QUESTION 14

Rate your level of knowledge about the following:

How to craft a successful presentation

Answer (select one):

- ☐ No knowledge
- ☐ Little knowledge
- ☑ Adequate knowledge
- ☐ Extraordinary knowledge

QUESTION 15

Rate your level of knowledge about the following:

How groups form and develop

Answer (select one):

- ☐ No knowledge
- ☑ Little knowledge
- ☐ Adequate knowledge
- ☐ Extraordinary knowledge

QUESTION 16

Rate your level of knowledge about the following:

Characteristics of highly effective peer education groups

Answer (select one):

- ☐ No knowledge
- ☐ Little knowledge
- ☑ Adequate knowledge
- ☐ Extraordinary knowledge

Understanding the Power, Roles, and Characteristics of Peer Educators

As you listen to the facilitator present information, add your notes to the outline below.

DEFINITIONS

- Peer: accessible and share an ability to influence eachother

- Peer educator: uses knowledge/skills to help peeo make healthy choices

cpe
Certified Peer Educator

FIVE ROLES OF A PEER EDUCATOR

- **Friend:**

- listen
- Resources
- Supportive / accountable

- **Educator:** Teach
  - awarness
- Resources

- **Activist:** Create positive change
- Partnership
- Bystander

- **Role model:** Lead healthy / balanced lives
- lead by example / Support other

- **Team member:** Be active member
  - Work w advisor
  - Support others

ETHICS AND INTEGRITY

- Ethics: Moral Principles that govern a Person's groups/behavior

- Integrity: honest/strong moral

FIVE PRINCIPLES OF INTEGRITY

- Autonomy: unique ✓

- Nonmaleficence: No harm ✓

- Beneficence: Good

- Justice: Fairness

- Fidelity: keeping Promiss

ACTIVITY: WHAT WOULD YOU DO?

Consider one or more of the following scenarios. Think about what you would do if you encountered this situation, based on the five moral principles we just discussed.

Scenario 1: You are planning an event and will be providing free food to attendees using your group's budget. You have a friend who cannot afford to buy food, and she asks you to order an extra pizza for her as part of your event. She has to work during the event and cannot attend. What do you do?

Scenario 2: You work retail at a local clothing store. Your friend walks in and sees a scarf for sale. He says that he wants it, but it is too expensive. He asks if you can ring it up using your employee discount, which is against store policy. What do you do?

Scenario 3: You consider yourself to be a friendly person; however, you just cannot stand Taylor. Taylor is always trying to "one up" you. You hear your friend Jesse saying negative things about Taylor's family, sexuality, and partner. What do you do?

ACTIVITY: GROUP DISCUSSION

- Which of Kitchener's (1984) ethical principles is easiest for you to adhere to? Which is the hardest?

- Which of the ethical principles do you think is most applicable to your work as a peer educator?

- How might knowing and striving to adhere to these principles as a student influence your professional development?

COMMON TRAPS FOR PEER EDUCATORS

- Trying to do too much:

  - highly active students fall into this trap
  - being busy
  - value someones time and see you can't be your best self

- Taking on something too big:

  - Can't handle by yourself
  - May be beyond ability
  - May need to refer to campus/community resources

- Internalizing the issue:

- Something about a situation triggers you
- You can't create mental boundary
between yourself + person

- Blurring the lines of integrity and ethics:

- No false promises of confidential/private

- work in unique situation

- agree to peer education

STRESS

- **Eustress:** Normal Stress
  - beneficial
  - Positive

- **Distress:** abnormal amt of stress can be overwhelming

ACTIVITY: STRESS MANAGEMENT BRAINSTORM

Use the space below to identify as many stress management techniques and behaviors as possible (both healthy and unhealthy).

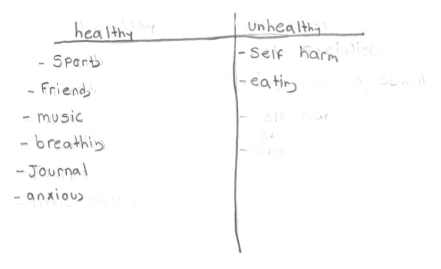

healthy	unhealthy
- Sports	- Self harm
- Friends	- eating
- music	- self har
- breathing	
- Journal	- eat
- anxious	

ACTIVITY: INDIVIDUAL REFLECTION

- How do you know when you are stressed?

  - anxious

  - sad

  - mad

- How does stress affect you as a student? As a peer educator?

  - Tired

  - unmotivated

- What do you do to manage your stress?

  - Journal
  - lift
  - sport
  - hang w friends
  - music

MODULE 1 REVIEW

- What is the definition of a peer? A peer educator?
- What are the traps of peer educators?
- What are the five roles of peer educators?

Describe the importance of self-care in your role as a peer educator.

MODULE 2

*Understanding Change
as a Peer Educator*

THE SOCIAL ECOLOGICAL MODEL (SIMPLIFIED)

- Individual: 1 on 1

- Targeted/group: Small group

- Community/population: Large group

STAGES OF CHANGE, OR TRANSTHEORETICAL, MODEL (SIMPLIFIED)

- **Precontemplation:** Unaware that change is needed
  - Bad doesn't outweigh good

- **Contemplation:** Change could be needed
  - eager to change
  - Doesn't know where to Start

- **Preparation:** Make Plan
  - Haven't started change
  - Other resources

- **Action:** Begin change
  - Make mistakes

- **Maintenance:** Change is Part of life.
  - have made change
  - inspire others
  - Can Fall back

ACTIVITY: SMALL-GROUP DISCUSSION OR INDIVIDUAL REFLECTION

In the space provided below, respond to the prompts related to change.

- Think of a change someone might want to make (e.g., exercising three times a week). How would you talk to someone differently depending on what stage of change her or she is in?

  Meet in middle

- Think of a change you have made or are trying to make. What stage are you in? What is it like being in that stage?

  3, Not bad

- What do you need to move forward or continue with your change?

  motivation

ROGERS' (2003) DIFFUSION OF INNOVATIONS MODEL

- Innovators: New Methods / ideas

- Early Adopters: interested in idea

- Early Majority: engaging

- Late Majority: waiting

- Laggards: Not w trends

HIGH-RISK BEHAVIOR

MODULE 2 REVIEW

- What are the three social ecological approaches to change making?
- What are the five Stages of Change?
- What are the five types of people according to Rogers' Diffusion of Innovations Model?
- What is a high-risk behavior?

MODULE 3

*Being an Effective Listener
as a Peer Educator*

ACTIVITY: FUZZY MEANINGS

As you read the words below, specify a number between 0 and 100 that best indicates the amount (percentage) of time that each word conveys.

- Often: 80 %

- Always: 100 %

- Sometimes: 50%

- Never: 0 %

- Usually: 70 %

- Most of the time: 90%

35

cpe
Certified Peer Educator

- Occasionally: 65%

- Seldom: 5%

- A lot: 80%

- Almost always: 95%

- Rarely: 5%

- Frequently: 60%

- Quite often: 70%

Group Discussion

- What did you learn from this activity?

We all understand things diff

- How does this activity affect your role as a peer educator?

Better communication

- How could this activity help you better communicate with others?

Clarifying

ACTIVITY: HOW TO MAKE A SANDWICH

Your facilitator will give you instructions for completing this activity, in which two volunteers will attempt to make a peanut butter and jelly sandwich.

Group Discussion

- What made this activity difficult?

- What might have made this task easier?

- How does this apply to your role as a peer educator?

WHY DO PEOPLE SEEK A LISTENER?

- Lonely/isolated:

- The only one:

- Not knowing where to begin:

- Dump and run:

- Wanting not to be judged:

EMPATHY VERSUS SYMPATHY

- Sympathy: Feeling for someone "Sorry"

  "Sorry"

- Empathy: Put yourself in someone's shoes

  feel w this

WHAT MAKES PEOPLE APPROACHABLE?

- What is their demeanor?

- Will they understand?

- Will they have time?

- Will they tell anyone?

- Will they judge me?

ACTIVITY: TELEPHONE

The game begins when an individual at one end of the group is given a message by the facilitator. The first person in line then whispers the message into the second person's ear. The speaker can whisper the message only once and the listener cannot ask to have it repeated or ask any questions. Proceed with this process until the message reaches the last person. The last person in line will announce the message they heard.

Group Discussion

- What contributed to the message being changed?

- What obstacles made listening difficult?

- What are some skills a person should have to be an effective listener?

BARRIERS TO LISTENING

- Distractions:

- Listening environment:

- Letting the mind wander:

- Prejudging the speaker:

- Rushing to solve the issue:

- Showing signs of needing to leave

- Dismissing or invalidating feelings:

EXt barrier: Factor in envi make it diff to listn

int barrier: Factor that exist in the listner own thoughts and feeling

- **Enabling:** Creating and attempting a solution

Non verbal: gestures

verbal: words

TECHNIQUES FOR EFFECTIVE LISTENING

- Create a listening environment:

- Be mindful of your nonverbal communication:

- Practice mindfulness as a listener:

NONVERBAL COMMUNICATION

- Relaxed:

- Open:

- Lean in:

- Eye contact:

- Square up:

PRACTICE MINDFULNESS AS A LISTENER

- Be aware of attitudes, prejudices, beliefs, and emotions:

- Focus on listening to the speaker:

- Suspend personal judgments:

- Meet the person "where they are":

- Accept the person's right to their own choices:

- Refer if you can't be nonjudgmental:

ENCOURAGING PEOPLE TO SHARE

- "Still here" phrases:

- Bridges/links:

MOTIVATIONAL INTERVIEWING

- Open-ended questions:

- Affirmations:

- Reflective listening:

- Summaries:

Remember: You must meet the speaker "where they are."

ACTIVITY: LISTENING IN PRACTICE

Reflection Circle

Sit in a circle in small groups. Each group should pick one person to start the activity. That person will make a short statement, such as "I went to my biology class this morning." Another person will then paraphrase that statement using reflective listening. For example, "You're taking a science class this semester." After the reflection, that person will make a different statement of their own. Continue this cycle for 3 to 5 minutes.

Ask the Facilitator

One person in the class will come up with a problem faced by college students, such as homesickness, alcohol use, or poor grades. Each participant should talk to the facilitator (or to a designated person in your small group) from a listener's perspective by asking open-ended questions. Each student in the class or small group should ask at least one open-ended question before moving on.

Group Discussion

- Was this activity harder than you thought it would be?

- Why might this activity have been difficult?

- What are some ways you can practice these techniques and other active listening skills?

MODULE 3 REVIEW

- What is the difference between empathy and sympathy?
- What are some barriers to effective listening?
- How can we establish a good listening environment?
- What are the ROLES used in nonverbal communication?
- What is a "still here" phrase?
- What is motivational interviewing?

MODULE 4

*A Peer Educator's Role
as a Responder*

RESPONDING ON DIFFERENT LEVELS

- Individual or small-scale response:

  -Mental health

  -Coming out

  - Bias

- Community-level response:

  - Trauma

PLAN OF ACTION RESPONSE CHECKLIST

- Determine what you want to happen:

  — What

  — change / listening

47

- Determine why you want this to happen:

- Do a reality check:

- Make a plan:

- Commit to taking action:

- Plan the first step and first reward:

ACTIVITY: PLAN OF ACTION

Watch the video of two students walking through the Plan of Action checklist together. Take notes in the space below regarding what you feel was done well and what was not done well.

Steps	Notes on Steps
1. What do you want to have happen?	
2. Why do you want this to happen?	
3. Do a reality check.	
4. Make a plan.	
5. Commit to taking action.	
6. Plan the first step and the first reward.	

Group Discussion

- What did the peer educator do well? What did the peer educator not do well?

- Did the Plan of Action model seem effective? Why or why not?

- How might this model be helpful in your role as a peer educator?

CONFIDENTIALITY GUIDELINES

- Be honest:

- If you need to tell, tell a campus professional:

- Stop other peer educators from sharing confidential information:

- If you are unsure what to do, ask for help:

- Know your school policies:

REFERRALS AND CAMPUS RESOURCES

- Not all situations need a referral:

- It is possible to give too many referrals:

- The person has the right to refuse a referral:

- Gauge whether the person feels capable of following through:

- Make sure your referrals are correct:

ACTIVITY: CAMPUS RESOURCES BRAINSTORM

In the space below, reflect on the resources that you have used on campus and/or have heard of. What resources could be allies for you in your work as a peer educator?

CRISIS MANAGEMENT CYCLE

- Prevention and Mitigation:

- Planning:

- Response:

- Recovery:

- Learning:

RESPONSE ON CAMPUS

- **Title IX:** Gender based violence

- **Campus safety/police:** Public safety, Response

- **Counseling services:** Counselor

- Case management: Student issues/concerns

- Behavior intervention team (BIT): intervention for those in need

MODULE 4 REVIEW

- What are the five steps of the Crisis Management Cycle?
- What are the six steps to making a plan of action?
- What is a behavior intervention team?

MODULE 5

*Bystander Intervention
as a Peer Education Technique*

WHAT IS A BYSTANDER?

- Bystander: Observer of a situation w harmful acts

- Active bystander: intervenes

- Passive bystander: does not intervene

*Depends on situation

cpe
Certified Peer Educator

ACTIVITY: PERSONAL BYSTANDER HISTORY

Think of a time when you could have been an engaged and active bystander but were not.

- Why did you not react?

When 2 People I was both friends with were fighting

I didn't want to be in the middle of Conflict

- How could you have acted?

I could have told them to work it out together.

BARRIERS TO ACTIVE BYSTANDING

- Negative experience:

- Support:

- Risk:

- Gender, cultural, and social roles:

- Emotional state:

- Peer pressure:

- Self-confidence:

AMBIVALENCE TO ACTIVE BYSTANDING

- Social influence: Behavior / Reaction

- Evaluation apprehension: Negative Judgment

- Diffusion of responsibility: Someone else address's Situation

- Pluralistic ignorance: No one else believes as we do

THE FIVE-STEP DECISION-MAKING MODEL

1. Recognize the problem:

2. Interpret the problem:

3. Take personal responsibility:

4. Decide how to assist:

5. Take action:

INTERVENING GUIDELINES

- Be ready: Prepare mentally/physically

- Identify the behavior: Call out behavior not person

- Appeal to principles: Most people are good people

- Set limits: Don't cross a line

- Find allies: Strength in numbers

- Be persistent: Don't get dissappointed

MODULE 5 REVIEW

- What is the difference between an active and a passive bystander? *[handwritten: intervenes   Does not]*
- What are some reasons why someone would not intervene in a situation?
- What are the five steps of deciding to intervene?

MODULE 6

Intrapersonal Applications of Identity as a Peer Educator

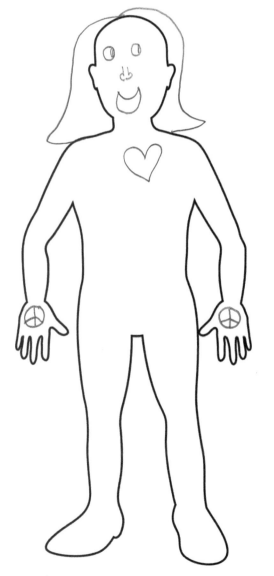

ACTIVITY: IDENTITY MINDSET

The person outline (to right) allows you to think about who you are and how you want the world to see you. With this person outline, please draw how you want the world to see you. Be as creative as you desire. You may wish to include parts of your identity that make you "you," characteristics or qualities that are a metaphor for your values, or social identities that define who you are.

cpe
Certified Peer Educator

WHAT IS IDENTITY?

- Identity: Qualities that make up a Person

- Personal identity: aspects of you

- Social identity: Societal views

- Disenfranchisement: Deprived of a rbht

- Bias: Prejudice views

ACTIVITY: PERSONAL IDENTITY WHEEL

To the best of your ability, complete the personal identity wheel (below). You are encouraged to allow yourself to be vulnerable and share your true feelings and thoughts; however, share only what you feel empowered to reveal.

SOCIAL IDENTITIES: THE D9+

- Ability status: Mental / Physical disability

- Age: Current age

- Sex assigned at birth: Male / Female

- Gender identity and expression: Society trend along w Feminism, Masculinity

- National origin: Original Place

- Race and ethnicity: Category of Physical apperance
- Skin, hair

    Common language, experiences

- Religious affiliation: Denomination of belonging

- Sexual Orientation: Choosing a Partner

- Socioeconomic status: Financial status and structure

Plus: Body size etc...

Remember: Your identities don't exist in a silo.

Intersectionality: Identities work together

ACTIVITY: SOCIAL IDENTITY WHEELS

To the best of your ability, complete the social identity wheel (below). You are encouraged to allow yourself to be vulnerable and share your true feelings and thoughts; however, share only what you feel empowered to reveal.

MODULE 6 REVIEW

- What is the difference between a personal and a social identity?
- What are the D9+ social identities?
- How would you define disenfranchisement and inequality?
- What is intersectionality?

MODULE 7

*Programming Strategies
for Peer Educators*

ACTIVITY: CASE STUDIES

In small groups, discuss the case studies below. Identify how you would handle the situation, and who you think is right. Afterward, share with the larger group what you discussed.

- Ken is a doctor who is treating Sean, a chronic pain patient. Sean wants to try a treatment that hasn't been researched very much, but his friends have told him that it worked for them. Ken believes the treatment is ineffective and a waste of time because there is no research to support it; he would rather have Sean stick to traditional, more well-researched avenues. Who is right? How would you manage the disagreement?

- Holly is a peer educator and the president of her peer education group. She is helping some newer members of the group plan a program. They want to do a presentation on alcohol education that includes a crashed car display and "drunk goggles" to illustrate the effects of driving under the influence. Holly knows that these methods haven't been shown to have any effect on behavior change and wants her peers to pick other activities and displays. The other peer educators believe these displays work best to get students to pay attention to their message. Who is right? How would you manage the disagreement?

EVIDENCE-BASED PRACTICES

- Tier 1

  - know Practice works

- Tier 2: general pop, little evidence

- Tier 3: Strong evidence, little evidence

- Tier 4: Practice is not effective

FOUR CORNERSTONES OF A PRESENTATION

- Know yourself.
    - o Your style: Describe the speaking or presenting style you are comfortable with.

    - o Your skills: Make a list of your skills, such as acting, humor, or artistic ability.

    - o Your strengths and weaknesses: Make a list of your strengths and the areas you would like to improve.

- Know your material.
    - o Identify your topic.

    - o Identify how you will research this topic.

    - o Identify some reliable sources of data and statistics for your topic.

- Know your audience.
  - o Identify some pieces of information you would want to know about your audience before presenting.

- Know your purpose.
  - o Identify what information you will provide.

  - o Identify how you plan to change student attitudes about the issue.

  - o Identify how you will teach students skills to deal with the issue.

THREE PARTS OF A PRESENTATION

- Creating space: Warm up

- Delivery: variety

- Conclusion: Thanks audienc

NOMINAL GROUP PROCESS: PART 1

- Be clear about what problem you are trying to address.
- Make a list of suggestions on your own.
- There are no wrong answers; quantity, not quality.

Use the space below to individually generate as many ideas as possible for your group's chosen brainstorm.

-abt NDCL

- Sport

-activits

NOMINAL GROUP PROCESS: PART 2

- Share answers with the group one by one.
- There are no right or wrong answers.
- Suspend judgment and evaluation.

NOMINAL GROUP PROCESS: PART 3

- Once you've brainstormed, evaluate the responses.
- Eliminate repeated answers.
- Group like concepts together.
- Eliminate responses that won't lead to an effective solution.
- Discuss which of the remaining responses will work best.

EVENT PLANNING CONSIDERATIONS

- Assessment:

- Learning outcomes:

ACTIVITY: WRITING A LEARNING OUTCOME

- Learning outcomes should be measurable, specific, and "person first."
- Think of the SWiBAT (Students Will Be Able To) Model.

Below are some sample verbs you can use as you are creating learning outcomes.

- Analyze
- Apply
- Classify
- Communicate
- Construct
- Create
- Define
- Demonstrate
- Describe
- Design
- Distinguish
- Evaluate
- Explain
- Identify
- Illustrate
- Justify
- Modify
- Organize
- Participate
- Produce
- Recognize
- Review
- Specify
- Summarize
- Translate
- Write

Use the space below to write one or two learning outcomes related to the topic you came up with through the nominal group process.

EVENT PLANNING CONSIDERATIONS (CONTINUED)

- Budget:

- Fundraising:

- Location:

- Timing (setup, cleanup):

- Food:

- Incentives:

- Presentation/entertainment:

- Marketing:

- Evaluation

EVALUATION

When writing an evaluation, consider the following tips and tricks to make them more effective:

- Always evaluate your programs and presentations—this gives you great feedback moving forward.
- Consider when you want to administer the survey and what tool you will use to do so.
- Derive your evaluation from your learning outcomes.
- Ask both quantitative and qualitative questions.
- Consider how you'll use your data afterward.

Use the space on the following pages to write at least one quantitative and one qualitative evaluation question for your event.

Sample quantitative question:

To what extent do you agree with the following statement:

> *This program has outlined ways that I can be an effective peer educator.*

Sample quantitative question options:
- Strongly disagree
- Disagree
- Agree
- Strongly agree

Quantitative Question 1:

Quantitative question options:

1. _____

2. _____

3. _____

4. _____

Quantitative Question 2:

Quantitative question options:

1. _____

2. _____

3. _____

4. _____

Sample qualitative question:

What skills of effective peer educators do you still have questions about?

Qualitative Question 1:

Qualitative Question 2:

ACTIVITY: EVENT PLANNING ACTION GUIDE

Use the following worksheet to assist your group in planning an event. As you discuss each item, write down short notes about the event.

Event Name: Banana Scavenger hunt
Goal: Get People aquainted to classes

Sponsors & Contributors:
1.
2.
3.
4.

Budget:

Date:	**Time:** Liontime	**Location:** NDCL hallway
		Reservation & Cost:

Audiovisual Equipment & Costs:
1.
2.
3.

Food Needs & Costs:

1.

2.

3.

1. Speaker/Presenter Contact Information & Cost:	2. Speaker/Presenter Contact Information & Cost:

Information Needed for Media, Marketing, and Promotions:

Publicity/Marketing Contacts:

Contact Name	Contact Phone/Fax	Contact E-mail	Advertising Cost
1.			
2.			
3.			

How Attendees Will Evaluate the Event:	How We Will Evaluate the Event:
1.	1.
2.	2.
3.	3.
4.	4.

MODULE 7 REVIEW

- What are some good verbs to use when writing learning outcomes?
- What three parts make up a successful presentation?
- What are the four cornerstones to a great presentation?
- In what ways can you evaluate a program/presentation?

Group Development and
Moving Forward

ACTIVITY: GROUP ROLE INVENTORY

Complete the following inventory. When you are done, add up your scores using the template below.

Number of A's	Number of B's	Number of C's	Number of D's
		5	

1. How do you deal with conflict in a group?

    a. I put together a plan for how we will work together differently to mitigate the conflict.

    b. I remind people of the tasks they've been assigned and try to get back to work.

    c. I talk to people to get an idea of their concerns and try to find common ground.

    d. I give people a clear vision of what we can accomplish if we work well together.

83

2. What is your favorite part of group work?

    a. Mapping out the steps we need to take to achieve our goal

    b. Meeting goals and deadlines and checking off my to-do list

    c. Meeting and building relationships with my teammates

    d. Presenting and/or marketing the final product

3. What is most important to you when you are in a leadership role?

    a. A clear mission and concrete objectives

    b. Constant progress toward our goal

    c. Healthy, positive relationships within the team

    d. Showcasing the team's excellent work with others outside the team

4. What frustrates you the most when working in a group?

    a. When my teammates deviate from the plan we agreed on

    b. When my teammates procrastinate

    c. When my teammates argue excessively

    d. When my teammates can't see the broader implications of our work

5. What is your biggest strength as a team member?

    a. Planning and organizing

    b. Taking action and getting things done

    c. Building positive relationships that help us work better together

    d. Publicizing my team's successes

ACTIVITY: LEADERSHIP VERSUS FOLLOWERSHIP REFLECTION

Individually reflect on the following questions, then discuss your thoughts in small groups.

- What is the difference between a leader and a follower?

- What qualities make a good leader? A good follower?

- Who is more important to a group's success, a leader or a follower? Why?

- How do groups choose or identify leaders?

CYCLE OF GROUP FORMATION

- Forming: Create identity
    - Want to be accepted
    - avoid Conflict/Controversy

- **Storming:** Conflict arises
  - Conflict is normal/important
  - Members struggle w ideas, work styls, personalits

- **Norming:** Identites are formed
  - New conflics are welcomed
  - Members: Complete tasks, Produce outcons, have impact disagree, high energy, Resolve conflict

- **Performing:**

- **Adjourning:** People added/leave
  - New leadership/mission
  - Cycle
  - Celebrate goals

MISSION AND VISION

- **Mission:** Focus on today
  - Drives organization
  - goals

- **Vision:** Focus on future
  - Future of organization

ACTIVITY: WRITING A MISSION STATEMENT AND A VISION STATEMENT

Use the space below to work together with your small group to write a mission statement and a vision statement for your peer education group. If the group already has a mission and vison, talk with your group about them and think about what changes you might make.

SEVEN HABITS OF HIGHLY EFFECTIVE PEER EDUCATION GROUPS

- Strong, diverse membership: Multiple talents
  - Diverse idea, skills
  - group lacks, recruit

- Well-trained peers:

- Promote positive images:
  - Role model
  - Safe choices

- Active advisement:
  - Student wellness
  - Mentor
  - Work w people

- Branding:

- Administrative support: academic mission

- Student ownership:

ROLES OF AN ADVISOR

- Consultant: Guides student

- Director: Develop programs

- Supervisor: hire/Fire

- Administrator: Promote educatin

MODULE 8 REVIEW

- What are the five steps in the cycle of group formation?
- What is the difference between a mission and a vision?
- What are seven characteristics of highly effective peer education groups?
- What are the four roles of a strong peer education advisor?

identity: Blue Color

APPENDIX A

Glossary

MODULE 1

Ethics: Moral principles that govern a person's or group's behavior

Eustress: Normal stress, which can be beneficial or positive

Distress: An abnormal amount of stress, which can become overwhelming

Integrity: The quality of being honest and having strong moral principles; moral uprightness

Peer: Someone who is of equal standing with you in a group and shares a similar level of influence

Peer educator: Someone who maximizes their knowledge and skills to encourage their peers to make healthy (or healthier) choices

MODULE 2

High-risk behavior: A behavior that is highly probable with a target population, as well as highly impactful in its consequences

MODULE 3

Sympathy: Feeling "for" someone; a sense of feeling sorry for them

Empathy: Attempting to put yourself in someone else's shoes; essentially feeling "with" them

MODULE 4

Clery Act: The requirement of campuses to report crimes and other data out to the campus community on an annual basis, as well as to maintain a robust recordkeeping system while also notifying students in a timely manner of incidents that occur on campus. Sexual assault peer health educators, for example, may be faced with Clery Act requirements.

FERPA: Allows individuals on college and university campuses the right to keep their educational records confidential, meaning that many educational records, including grades and class standing, must remain confidential among campus professionals and constituents outside campus without an explicit "need to know"

HIPAA: Focuses on one's right to privacy regarding health and medical conditions. Although this mostly affects medical professionals, peer health educators can sometimes blur the lines of health professionals and students may think they are confidential sources.

Title IX: As a legal requirement, it focuses on discrimination. When incidents that involve a protected class occur on campus, a Title IX investigation is often launched.

MODULE 5

Active bystander: Someone who intervenes in a potentially harmful situation

Bystander: An observer of a situation in which a friend or stranger may experience harmful or hurtful acts

Passive bystander: Someone who does not intervene in the aforementioned situation

MODULE 6

The D9+

- **Ability status**: One's ability to act and function in the world as designed without additional assistance
- **Age**: How old someone is; what generational group her or she falls into
- **Sex assigned at birth**: One's anatomical genitalia
- **Gender identity and expression**: One's internal identity and how it is expressed; may or may not align with sex assigned at birth
- **National origin**: The country or political state that an individual is from
- **Race and ethnicity**
    - ◊ **Race**: How one is viewed and categorized by the world, based on physical manifestations of genetic characteristics
    - ◊ **Ethnicity**: Cultural and ancestral factors in one's upbringing

- **Religious affiliation**: One's belief (or lack of belief) in an organized religion
- **Sexual orientation**: With sex and gender as supporting factors, how one identifies and has sexual activity with a partner
- **Socioeconomic status**: Class status, based on factors including income, education level, and occupation
- **Identity**: The qualities, beliefs, and so on that make a particular person or group different from others
- **Personal identity**: Identities that do not historically elicit disenfranchisement or bias
- **Social identity**: Identities that are socially constructed and elicit some sort of bias and hierarchy of privilege

MODULE 7

Qualitative data: Open-ended responses

Quantitative data: Deals with numbers as data

Worksheets

PLAN OF ACTION (RESPONSE CHECKLIST)

Steps	*Notes on Steps*
1. What do you want to have happen?	
2. Why do you want this to happen?	
3. Do a reality check.	
4. Make a plan.	
5. Commit to taking action.	
6. Plan the first step and the first reward.	

EVENT PLANNING ACTION GUIDE

Use the following worksheet to assist your group in planning an event. As you discuss each item, write down short notes about the event.

Event Name:

Goal:

Sponsors & Contributors:

1.

2.

3.

4.

Budget:

Date:	Time:	Location:
		Reservation & Cost:

Audiovisual Equipment & Costs:

1.

2.

3.

Food Needs & Costs:

1.

2.

3.

1. Speaker/Presenter Contact Information & Cost:	2. Speaker/Presenter Contact Information & Cost:

Information Needed for Media, Marketing, and Promotions:

Publicity/Marketing Contacts:

	Contact Name	Contact Phone/Fax	Contact E-mail	Advertising Cost
1.				
2.				
3.				

How Attendees Will Evaluate the Event:	How We Will Evaluate the Event:
1.	1.
2.	2.
3.	3.
4.	4.

Mission

Using the guidelines listed on page 51, write down your mission statement.

_____

_____

_____

_____

Vision

Using the guidelines listed on page 51, write down your vision statement.

_____

_____

_____

_____

EVALUATION WRITING TEMPLATE

In the space below, practice writing an evaluation based on your mock program.

Sample quantitative question:

To what extent do you agree with the following statement:

This program has outlined ways that I can be an effective peer educator.

Quantitative question options:

- Strongly disagree
- Disagree
- Agree
- Strongly agree

Quantitative Question 1:

_____

Quantitative question options:

_____   _____   _____   _____

Quantitative Question 2:

_____

Quantitative question options:

_____   _____   _____   _____

Quantitative Question 3:

_____

Quantitative question options:

_____   _____   _____   _____

Sample qualitative question:

What skills of effective peer educators do you still have questions about?

Qualitative question space:

_____

_____

Qualitative Question 1:

_____

Qualitative question space:

_____

_____

Qualitative Question 2:

_____

Qualitative question space:

_____

_____

Qualitative Question 3:

_____

Qualitative question space:

_____

_____

APPENDIX C

Module-End Reflection Activities

We understand that there are many opportunities for reflection throughout the CPE Training Program. As you continue your journey as peer educators, you may find that you need to refresh yourself on various pieces of your peer education training. The following pages include reflection questions and activities for you from each module. We encourage you to utilize these throughout the year to help strengthen and reinforce your peer education training.

MODULE 1 REFLECTION ACTIVITIES

Choose one or more of the following questions and write your answer(s).

1. On a scale of 1 (low) to 5 (high), rate yourself on how well you are performing in each of these peer educator roles.

- Friend:

- Educator:

cpe
Certified Peer Educator

- Activist:

- Role model:

- Team member:

    a. In which of the roles do you want to improve? How can you improve?

    b. When and in what ways might peers be a helpful part of the educational team?

2. Do you think being a peer educator helps you live a healthy lifestyle? Why or why not?

3. How is your behavior consistent with the mission of your peer education group?

4. What traps of peer educators are you sometimes likely to fall into? How can you avoid this?

MODULE 2 REFLECTION ACTIVITY

Choose a behavior you want to change and make the commitment to change for a month. This could be a physical health behavior, time management, social interactions, and the like. In the space below, create a plan to make the behavior change. You may want to consider the smaller steps involved in the process, as well as the stages of change you will go through.

At the end of the month, review the plan and see how it went. Reflect on the following questions:

- Did you change?

- What was hard to change?

- What was easier than expected?

- Did you seek help/resources?

- Who else did you involve in the change?

- If you "fell off," did you "get back on"?

- How does this apply to the Stages of Change model?

- How will this help you influence others to make a change?

MODULE 3 REFLECTION ACTIVITIES

Choose one or more of the following questions and write your answer(s).

1. Create a list of three closed-ended questions and convert them into open-ended questions. For example:

   - Closed-ended question: Do you want to break up with him/her?

   - Open-ended question: Where do you see your relationship going?

2. Read the statements below. For each statement, write an open-ended question that could be asked as a follow-up to the statement.

   - I am so tired of midterms!

   - It seems like all my friends are in relationships but me.

- This may sound stupid, but I'm still a virgin.

3. Make a list of actions you plan to take to be an effective listener.

MODULE 4 REFLECTION ACTIVITIES

Choose one or more of the following questions and write your answer(s).

1. Answer the following responding and referral reflection questions:

- How does a peer educator know whether to make a referral?

- How do we help a student come to their own conclusion?

- Why does one make a referral?

2. Answer the following resource knowledge self-reflection questions:

- For what issues on campus do you know the campus or community resources?

- For which issues do you need to find the campus or community resources?

- How will you find this information? Who can you ask? What directories or websites will provide the information needed?

MODULE 5 REFLECTION ACTIVITIES

Choose one or more of the following questions and write your answer(s).

Think about the past month. Read through the list of actions below and record how many times you performed any of them. Next, answer the self-reflection questions on intervening.

1. In the past month, how many times have you done the following:

   - Encouraged someone to seek help?

   - Encouraged someone to call a counselor or medical professional?

   - Called the police or public safety department about a safety issue?

   - Intervened when someone was too intoxicated to give consent and was being taken advantage of?

   - Confronted a friend or peer about alcohol abuse?

   - Confronted a friend or peer about high-risk behavior?

   - Intervened when a friend or peer used sexist, racist, or demeaning language?

2. Reflect on your answers to the intervening questions you answered above.

- After answering the questions above, what surprises you?

- If you had an opportunity to do one of the items above but did not, what held you back?

- What can you do to increase the number of times you intervene?

MODULE 6 REFLECTION ACTIVITIES

Choose one or more of the following questions and write your answer(s).

1. What are some of the ways people might perceive you, and how might they be wrong?

2. What aspects of your personality or background do you sometimes feel others may be judgmental about?

3. How do you take this knowledge and incorporate it into your peer education efforts?

4. How do we assess our own group's diversity? Are we embracing our own diversity? Are we reflective of our campus's/community's diversity? What can we do to ensure that we reflect this diversity on campus?

cpe
Certified Peer Educator

MODULE 7 REFLECTION ACTIVITIES

Choose one or more of the following questions and write your answer(s).

Program Planning Skills Assessment

Think about programs you have helped plan in the past and answer the following questions:

1. What are your planning strengths?

2. What planning areas can you improve?

3. What are three steps you can take to improve these planning areas?

Best and Worst Presentations

Write your answers to the following questions:

1. Describe the best presentation you have ever attended. Because of the presentation, did you change a behavior or the way you thought about an issue? What about the presentation made such an impact on you?

2. Describe the worst presentation you have ever attended. Why did the presentation leave you with a negative impression?

3. Describe what you want to be sure to include in a presentation you develop. Use what you learned in this module, as well as what you wrote in the previous two questions, to identify what you should (or should not) include in a presentation.

MODULE 8 REFLECTION ACTIVITIES

Write your answers to the following questions:

Cycle of Group Formation

1. In what stage of the cycle of group formation is your peer education group?

2. What is happening that leads you to this conclusion?

3. In what stage would you like to see your group?

Mission and Vision

1. What mission-driven activities does your group do?

2. Which parts of your group's mission or mission-driven activities align with the mission of your institution or department? Which do not?

APPENDIX D

Selected Resources

Adamson, A., & Sorell, M. (2007). *BrandSimple: How the best brands keep it simple and succeed*. Hampshire, England: Palgrave Macmillan.

Allen, D. R., & Trimble, R. W. (1993). Identifying and referring troubled students: A primer for academic advisors. *NACADA Journal, 13*(2), 34–41.

Amodeo, J., & Wentworth, K. (1995). Self-revealing communication: A vital bridge between two worlds. In J. Stewart (Ed.), *Bridges not walls* (6th ed.) (pp. 206–210). New York, NY: McGraw-Hill.

Astin, A. (1993). *What matters in college: Four critical years revisited*. San Francisco, CA: Jossey-Bass.

Barkan, S. E. (2011). *Sociology: Understanding and changing the social world, comprehensive edition.* Retrieved from https://saylordotorg.github.io/text_sociology-understanding-and-changing-the-social-world-comprehensive-edition/s13-race-and-ethnicity.html

Benton, S. A., & Benton, S. L. (Eds.). (2006). *College student mental health*. Washington, DC: NASPA–Student Affairs Administrators in Higher Education.

Berkowitz, A. D. (2006, October 19–22). *Understanding the role of bystander behavior*. Presented at the U.S. Department of Education's 20th Annual Meeting on Alcohol and Other Drug Abuse Prevention and Violence Prevention in Higher Education, Arlington, VA.

Bresciani, M. J., Zelna, C. L., & Anderson, J. A. (2004). *Assessing student learning and development*. Washington, DC: NASPA–Student Affairs Administrators in Higher Education.

Burley-Allen, M. (1995). *Listening: The forgotten skill: A self-teaching guide*. Hoboken, NJ: John Wiley & Sons.

Chavez, A. F., & Sanlo, R. (Eds.). (2013). *Identity and leadership: Informing our lives, informing our practice*. Washington, DC: NASPA–Student Affairs Administrators in Higher Education.

Chickering, A. W., & Reisser, L. (1993). *Education and identity* (2nd ed.). San Francisco, CA: Jossey-Bass.

Cimini, M. D., & Rivero, E. M. (2018). *Promoting behavioral health and reducing risk among college students: A comprehensive approach*. New York, NY: Routledge.

D'Andrea, V. J., & Salovey, P. (1996). *Peer counseling: Skills, ethics, and perspectives* (2nd ed.). Palo Alto, CA: Science and Behavior Books.

Dimeff, L., Baer, J., Kirklahan, D., & Marlatt, G. (1999). *Brief alcohol screening and intervention for college students: A harm reduction approach*. New York, NY: The Guilford Press.

Egan, G. (2006). *Exercises in helping skills: To accompany the skilled helper* (8th ed.). Pacific Grove, CA: Wadsworth.

Ellison, S. S. (2002). *Take the war out of words: The art of powerful non-defensive communication*. Berkeley, CA: Bay Tree.

Ender, S. C., & Newton, F. B. (2000). *Students helping students: A guide for peer educators on college campuses*. San Francisco, CA: Jossey-Bass.

Evans, N. J., Forney, D. S., & Guido-DiBrito, F. (1998). *Student development in college: Theory, research, and practice*. San Francisco, CA: Jossey-Bass.

Fabiano, P. M. (1994). From personal health into community action: Another step forward in peer health education. *Journal of American College Health, 43*(3), 115–121.

Feldstein, S. W., & Forcehimes, A. A. (2007). Motivational interviewing with underage college drinkers: A preliminary look at the role of empathy and alliance. *American Journal of Drug and Alcohol Abuse, 33*(5), 737–746.

Gaskins, P. F. (1999). *What are you? Voices of mixed-race young people*. New York, NY: Macmillan.

Glanz, K., Rimer, B. K., & Viswnath, K. (2008). *Health behavior and health education: Theory, research, and practice* (4th ed.). San Francisco, CA: Jossey-Bass.

Green, L. W., & Kreuter, M. W. (2005). *Health program planning: An educational and ecological approach* (4th ed.). New York, NY: McGraw-Hill Higher Education.

Harper, K. S., Paterson, B. G., & Zdziarski, E. L., II (Eds.). (2006). *Crisis management: Responding from the heart*. Washington, DC: NASPA–Student Affairs Administrators in Higher Education.

Harper, R., & Wilson, N. L. (2010). *More than listening: A casebook for using counseling skills in student affairs work*. Washington, DC: NASPA–Student Affairs Administrators in Higher Education.

Harper, S. R. (Ed.). (2008). *Creating inclusive campus environments for cross-cultural learning and student engagement*. Washington, DC: NASPA–Student Affairs Administrators in Higher Education.

Hatcher, S. L. (Ed.). (1995). *Peer programs on the college campus: Theory, training, and the voice of peers*. San Jose, CA: Resource.

Hemphill, B. O., & Labanc, B. H. (Eds.). (2010). *Enough is enough: A student affairs perspective on preparedness and response to a campus shooting*. Washington, DC: NASPA–Student Affairs Administrators in Higher Education.

Herbst, P. (1997). *The color of words: An encyclopedic dictionary of ethnic bias in the United States*. Yarmouth, ME: Intercultural Press.

Hill, C. E. (2004). *Helping skills: Facilitating exploration, insight, and action* (2nd ed.). Washington, DC: American Psychological Association.

Hu, S., & Kuh, G. D. (2003). Diversity experiences and college student learning and personal development. *Journal of College Student Development, 44*(3), 320–334.

Kadison, R., & DiGeronimo, T. F. (2005). *College of the overwhelmed: The campus mental health crisis and what to do about it*. San Francisco, CA: Jossey-Bass.

Karriker, J. (2005). Cyclical group development and interaction-based leadership emergence in autonomous teams: An integrated model. *Journal of Leadership and Organizational Studies, 11*, 54–64.

Keeling, R. P. (Ed.). (2004). *Learning reconsidered: A campus-wide focus on student experience*. Washington, DC: American College Personnel Association and National Association of Student Personnel Administrators.

Keeling, R. P. (Ed.). (2004). *Learning reconsidered 2: Implementing a campus-wide focus on the student experience*. Washington, DC: American College Personnel Association, Association of College and University Housing Officers–International, Association of College Unions International, National Academic Advising Association, National Association for Campus Activities, National Association of Student Personnel Administrators, & National Intramural-Recreational Sports Association.

Keilburg, C., & Keilburg, M. (2008). *Me to we: Finding meaning in a material world*. New York, NY: Simon & Schuster.

Kitchener, K. S. (1984). Intuition, critical evaluation and ethical principles: The foundation for ethical decisions in counseling psychology. *Counseling Psychologist, 12*, 43–55.

Kohn, S., & O'Donnell, V. (2007). *6 habits of highly effective teams*. Franklin Lakes, NJ: The Career Press.

Komives, S. R., & Wagner, W. (2009). *Leadership for a better world: Understanding the social change model of leadership development* (2nd ed.). San Francisco, CA: Jossey-Bass.

Komives, S. R., Mainella, F. C., Longerbeam, S. D., Osteen, L., & Owen, J. E. (2006). A leadership identity development model: Applications from a grounded theory. *Journal of College Student Development, 47*(4), 401–418.

Lake, L. (2008). *What is branding and how important is it to your marketing strategy?* Retrieved from http://marketing.about.com/cs/brandmktg/a/whatisbranding.htm

Lake, P. F. (2011). *Foundations of higher education law and policy*. Washington, DC: NASPA–Student Affairs Administrators in Higher Education.

Landow, M. V. (Ed.). (2006). *College students: Mental health and coping strategies*. Hauppauge, NY: Nova Science.

Latané, B., & Darley, J. M. (1970). *Century Psychology Series: The unresponsive bystander: Why doesn't he help?* New York, NY: Appleton-Century Crofts.

Lencioni, P. (2002). *The five dysfunctions of a team: A leadership fable*. San Francisco, CA: Jossey-Bass.

Lowry, R. (2000). Physical activity, food choice, and weight management goals and practices among U.S. college students. *American Journal of Preventive Medicine, 18*(1), 18–27.

Marlatt, G. A., & Witkiewitz, K. (2002). Harm reduction approaches to alcohol use: Health promotion, prevention, and treatment. *Addictive Behavior, 27*(6), 867–886.

McCarthy, P., & Hatcher, C. (2002). *Presentation skills: The essential guide for students*. Thousand Oaks, CA: Sage.

McNeill, A. (2004). Harm reduction. *British Medical Journal, 328*, 885–887.

Miller, W. R., & Rollnick, S. (2002). *Motivational interviewing: Preparing people for change*. New York, NY: Guilford Press.

Paritzky, R. S. (1981). Training peer counselors: The art of referral. *Journal of College Student Personnel, 22*(6), 528–532.

Peale, N. V., & Blanchard, K. (1988). *The power of ethical management*. New York, NY: Harper Collins.

Perkins, H. W. (1995). Prevention through correcting misperceptions of alcohol and other drug norms: Notes on the state of the field. *Catalyst, 1*(3), 1–2.

Perkins, H. W. (2006). *A brief summary of social norms theory and the approach to promoting health*. Retrieved from http://alcohol.hws.edu/SocialNormsPrimer.html

Petress, K. C. (1999). Listening: A vital skill. *Journal of Instructional Psychology, 26*(4), 261–263.

Prochaska, J. O., Velicer, W. F., Rossi, J. S., Goldstein, M. G., Marcus, B. H., Rakowski, W., . . . Rosenbloom, D. (1994). Stages of change and decisional balance for twelve problem behaviors. *Health Psychology, 13*, 39–46.

Ries, A., & Ries, L. (1998). *22 immutable laws of branding*. New York, NY: HarperCollins.

Rogers, E. M. (2003). *Diffusion of innovations* (5th ed). New York, NY: Free Press.

Ross, S. E., Bradley, C. N., & Heckert, T. M. (1999). Sources of stress among college students. *College Student Journal, 33,* 312–318.

Rothenberg, P. S. (2007). *Race, class and gender in the United States: An integrated study* (7th ed.). New York, NY: Worth.

Russell, R. F. (2001). The role of values in servant leadership. *Leadership & Organization Development Journal, 22*(2), 76–84.

Sachs Hills, L. (2006). Becoming a better listener. *Journal of Medical Practice Management, 21*(6), 348–350.

Schultz, P. W., Nolan, J. M., Cialdini, R. B., Goldstein, N. J., & Griskevicius, V. (2007). The constructive, destructive, and reconstructive power of social norms. *Psychological Science, 18*(5), 429–434.

Sharkin, B. S., Plageman, P. M., & Mangold, S. L. (2003). College student response to peers in distress: An exploratory study. *Journal of College Student Development, 44*(5), 691–698.

Stark, M. (1994). *A primer on working with resistance*. Lanham, MD: Jason Aronson.

Stratton, K. (2001). *Clearing the smoke: Assessing the science base for tobacco harm reduction*. Washington, DC: National Academy of Sciences.

Sullivan, J. E. (2000). *The good listener*. Notre Dame, IN: Ave Maria Press.

Tatum, B. D. (2000). The ABC approach to creating climates of engagement on diverse campuses. *Liberal Education, 86*(4), 22–29.

Tollison, S. J., Lee, C. M., Neighbors, C., Neil, T. A., Olson, N. D., & Larimer, M. E. (2008). Questions and reflections: The use of motivational interviewing microskills in a peer-led brief alcohol intervention for college students. *Behavior Therapy, 39*(2), 183–194.

Tuckman, B. W. (1965). Developmental sequence in small groups. *Psychological Bulletin, 63*(6), 384–399. doi:10.1037/h0022100

U.S. Department of Health and Human Services, National Institutes of Health, National Institute on Alcohol Abuse and Alcoholism. (2007). *What colleges need to know: An update on college drinking research* (NIH Publication No. 07–5010). Retrieved from https://pubs.niaaa.nih.gov/publications/UpdateCollegeDrinking/1College_Bulletin-508_361C4E.pdf

Walter, S. T., & Baer, J. S. (2006). *Talking with college students about alcohol: Motivational strategies for reducing abuse.* New York, NY: Guilford Press.

Wawrzynski, M. R., LoConte, C. L., & Straker, E. J. (2011). Learning outcomes for peer educators: The national survey on peer education. In L. B. Williams (Ed.), *Emerging issues and practices in peer education* (New Directions for Student Services, No. 133, pp. 17–27). San Francisco, CA: Jossey-Bass.

Whitt, E. J., Edison, M. I., Pascarella, E. T., Terenzini, P. T., & Nora, A. (2001). Influences on students' openness to diversity and challenge in the second and third years of college. *The Journal of Higher Education, 72*(2), 172–204.

Witte, K., Meyer, G., & Martell, D. (2001). *Effective health risk messages.* Thousand Oaks, CA: Sage.

Zimmerman, G. L., Olsen, C. G., & Bosworth, M. F. (2000). A "stages of change" approach to helping patients change behavior. *American Family Physician, 61*(5), 1409–1416.

HELPFUL WEBSITES

Alan Berkowitz
Noted scholar on substance abuse, gender, diversity, and social norms

http://www.alanberkowitz.com

Begin to Set Personal Boundaries
Setting and maintaining healthy boundaries

http://www.oprah.com/article/spirit/knowyourself/ss_lybl_control_06/1

Bystander Effect
More on psychological phenomena related to bystander behavior

http://changingminds.org/explanations/theories/bystander_effect.htm

The Community Guide
Evidence-based recommendations for programs and policies to promote population health

http://www.thecommunityguide.org

EdChange

Professional development, scholarship, and activism for diversity, social justice, and community growth

http://www.edchange.org

Jackson Katz

Cocreator of the Mentors in Violence Program

http://www.jacksonkatz.com

MedlinePlus: Stress Management

Suggestions for stress management strategies

http://www.nlm.nih.gov/medlineplus/ency/article/001942.htm

National Social Norms Institute at the University of Virginia

Information on using a social norms approach to facilitate behavior change

http://www.socialnorms.org

Presentation Tips for Public Speaking

Introduction to public speaking and presentation skills

http://www.aresearchguide.com/3tips.html

Teaching Tolerance

A project of the Southern Poverty Law Center

http://www.tolerance.org

UCLA Special Events

Checklists for planning and budgeting

http://www.specialevents.ucla.edu/resources.html